Preventing Global Disaster
A Worldwide Message of Hope

Silver Anniversary Series

By David K. Ewen, M.Ed.

ISBN-13: 978-1717546814

ISBN-10: 1717546811

<u>Contents</u>

David K. Ewen, M.Ed.

About the Book

The book "Preventing Global Disaster" was first presented as a letter to the president of the United States in 2017 under a different title. The author's increasing work globally has prompted him to give the same message worldwide. The message is one of hope with guidelines for humankind to prevent disaster. Extinction can be avoided given the Models of Excellence provided in this book. Let's give our children a reason to live a long future of global community and worldwide cooperation. We can do it if we try.

About the Author

David K. Ewen, M.Ed. Has been in education after earning his master's degree in education in 1988. As a business owner since 1994, he first worked regionally in the Northeast area of the United States working with authors, business Leaders, and entrepreneurs. Today, Mr. Ewen is a field ambassador representing the United States and supporting educational needs in Asia, The Middle East and Europe working with youth, college students, professionals, and business leaders.

For many years, David has worked with different cultures and different age groups and has represented the United States well by providing educational support in the area of language development, business communications and entrepreneurial studies.

<u>Necessary</u>

The global arena is becoming more important in people's lives than ever before. With today's media technology, easier to see what is going on and the emotional impact can be closely felt. The facets of religion, economy, security, disease, energy, climate, tourism, and employment are common threads that interweave in various cultures around the world.

Social media, online gaming, broadcasting, and other technologies have provided a window into other cultures that that was not possible years ago.

International trade has allowed for an even spread of culture around the world. An example are the popular fast food restaurants founded in the United States that have been planted in Asia, The Middle East, and Europe. Pizza is not just for Italians and hamburgers are not just for Americans. Food is not the only cultural aspect that is being spread evenly. The impact of religion and the extremism with false roots from religion have emerged and become prominent conversation when discussing differences and similarities among cultures.

As an evolving global community, it is our responsibility as the human citizens of Earth to promote collaboration of best practices and methodology to improve lifestyle as our population increases on a planet that remains consistent in size. If we fail in that effort, then conflict results for the fight for resources will comparatively increase with the increase in our world population.

We as a community across cultures here on Earth have a responsibility to be at peace and work together as close Neighbors as our population increases and the availability of resources come in skip. Those resources ted be well-managed using technology and other methodologies so that the fight for those resources is not necessary. The goal is to reduce the need for a fight and to increase the need for sharing.   Although technology is needed such as growing crops in a drought, the innovation and creativity that technology gives will allow the sharing of ideas to avoid the fight for resources.

Trending Around the World

The very first significant International experience that I encountered was when I met my wife from Colombia. We married six months after we met each other. The dawn going to the immigration process from step one all the way through citizenship took years. With this, even as an American I can understand what other immigrants go through when trying to seek a better life in another country.

The first contract work with a foreign nation was as a copywriter for a company in India providing articles to Australia, the UK, Canada, and the United States. This experience gave me insight as to what countries are interested in and what is trending on people's minds around the world.

The first exposure to an overseas culture in a professional business atmosphere was with Japan contracting educational Services to NTT learning services. My assignment was to teach Japanese professionals and business leaders daily and business conversation that is relevant worldwide. In a group setting, I had the advantageous opportunity to learn different aspects of Japanese Society and culture.

As I was expanding my role internationally, I joined a firm

through a freelance contract with a company in China supporting consumers, college students, professionals, and business leaders. The importance of the Chinese experience grew when I became head teacher managing the English department for this institution. Today my work is with two large Chinese firms working with youth up through college graduates who are Business Leaders. This provides a broad experience into the culture of people.

At the same time my work in China have a growing, I started in Vietnam and the Middle East. It's only been recently that might work in Europe had begun in the year 2018. Today, the territory I reach is Asia, the Middle East, and Europe. On occasion, work with people in South America.

I have discovered that the older generation (as of 2018) is more rigid in cultural traditions then the emerging younger generation who are heading towards College. The new generation immerse in technology that gives them a window view of other cultures around the world. Their parents and grandparents did not grow up with the internet technology serving as a portal to other cultures. That being said, there is a a growing trend where culture is being blended in the areas of religion, food, and clothing. For example, I work with people from China using educational curriculum from China that talks about the story of Christmas. Many youths in Japanese have told me they prefer coffee compared to green tea. Although the cultural stereotypes may be in place those stereotypes are becoming less true overtime.

The technologies of broadcasting, online gaming, streaming content, and the internet are slowly turning the different cultures seen around the world into a more closely uniform culture. Not to say that the world will become one uniform culture. What is being Illustrated is that various cultures around the world are being understood, accepted, and I respected. Of course, there are the extremists that go outside of the cultural norm that are becoming more visible because resources are available for to become more visible. My experience is that the extremist will not overpower the peaceful directions a cultural acceptance.

<u>A Responsibility</u>

We have a responsibility in humankind to develop a global Behavior that allows our world community to flourish economically and in good wellbeing that includes health, education, and well-being. As cultural neighbors, it is our responsibility to accept the existence and the well-being the vehicles of respect and cooperation with a focus achieving excellence in that responsibility. As the world population grows and the technology increases bringing cultures closer together, we as a people and Global community must think differently than our closed-minded ancestors.

Our ancestors could afford to be close-minded if they chose to because of the convenience of distance and a separation of communication. There was no immediate need four cultural acceptance. Unfortunately, that think it went too far allowing for slavery and discrimination to take root in modern cultures. Although it is a slow process, the beginning stages of clearly identifying infringement on cultural rights is helping to protect victims of discriminatory abuse.

<u>Survival</u>

As a field ambassador representing the United States to other countries in education, I created the Seven Pillars representing the Models of Excellence. These pillars using the Holy Bible as a reference help administer the cultural acceptance necessary for humankind growing globally centered on a worldwide community that needs to live together using shared resources. Those resources in history are fought for to achieve dominance. Some examples are territory, energy resources, and antiquated beliefs. Fighting it's not the long-term ocean for survival of a growing population on a planet remaining the same size. Innovative and creative collaboration using technology and advanced methodologies is what will help humankind grow and survive. The Seven Pillars representing the Models of Excellence can help serve as a guide.

<u>A Warning and Solution</u>

The message contained in this book sent to the worldwide community as a fellow global citizen was first received at the White House on July 17 2017 to be shared with the president of the United States. I felt it as a responsibility to offer solutions based on biblical principles founded thousands of years ago.

As I spend more time working globally in Asia, the Middle East, Europe, south America, in the United States, I find necessary to present the same message presented to the president of the United States to the rest of the world. It is a responsibility to share biblical principles embedded in guidelines to help humankind flourish in a growing worldwide community.

Our world history shows within a smaller Global community. Our population expansion and the draining of resources no longer allows us to behave in the archaic and antiquated ways of our past. Our survival depends on a mindset of cultural acceptance using a guy to help us along the way. There are no alternative choices. It is a must that we work together for our survival. My belief is that technology will play a significant role. Currently the technology in place exist to complete our destruction. We must avoid this at all cost. It is necessary.

I choose to do more than just say we must survive. As a representative serving as a citizen of the United States and acting as a field Ambassador in education reaching nations in Asia, and Europe I am compelled to offer logical solutions produced with deep thought and found it through biblical principles.

<u>Models of Excellence</u>

There are seven pillars representing the Models of Excellence. They are the following:

(1) Motivation
(2) Organization
(3) Discipline
(4) Ethics
(5) Learning
(6) Strength
(7) Combination

The seventh pillar, "Combination" is a combination of the previous six pillars. Each can stand alone and combined with others.

Motivation

The first pillar called motivation is the get up and go attitude that is self-driven offering a reason for acting and behaving in a beneficial way. Motivation is void of a state of Slumber and laziness.

It is easy to be in a state of slumber and behave in a lazy way. It requires fortitude and perseverance to be motivated. This requires a desired focused attention to be void of a lazy behavior. This action is self-driven and not controlled or swayed by others. Motivation is a responsibility that is based on action.

We all have choices in life. The choice to accept and embrace motivation is ours alone. We can choose to accept it or deny it. Accepting it has rewards. Denying it has consequences. The choice determines the outcome of rewards or consequences.

In Proverbs 6:9 the scripture reads, "How long will you slumber, O sluggard? When will you rise from your sleep?

<u>Organization</u>

Having organization put structure in life so that there is a path toward an objective allowing for the reward of a goal to be achieved. Without organization, there is no road map to a goal because no goal exists. Those who have organization accomplish things that are beneficial to themselves and others. Without organization. There is miss-direction and a sense of unawareness. The result is a confusing state of mind. By having organization, there is understanding, assured behavior, incompetent awareness. This allows accomplishments and goals to be achieved.

In 1st Corinthians 14:40, the scripture reads, "Let all things be done decently and in order."

In Luke 14:28, the scripture reads, "For which of you, intending to build a tower, does not sit down first and count the cost, whether he has enough to finish it"

<u>Discipline</u>

Discipline is knowing the difference between what you must do compared to what you want to do. Sometimes what you want to do interferes with what you must do. Doing what you must do will never negatively impact what you want to do. Discipline is understanding priorities in life by recognizing what must be done. There is an understanding of consequences when priorities are not met. That understanding insurance that consequences are avoided resulting in priorities taking precedence in our lives. Discipline requires obedience to the focused attention of the priorities that must be done. It involves a constant awareness and action to fulfill priorities as necessary.

In Hebrews 12:11, the scripture reads, "Now no chastening seems to be joyful for the present, but painful; nevertheless, afterward it yields the peaceable fruit of righteousness to those who have been trained by it."

In Titus 1:8, the scripture reads, "but hospitable, a lover of what is good, sober-minded, just, holy, self-controlled,"

<u>Ethics</u>

Ethics is knowing the difference between right and wrong. By not having ethics, wrong can be committed without being aware that it is not right. There is a firm division between what is considered right and what is considered wrong. One way that is created is by the legal system. A more important way is what is inherently understood and expected within Humanity. The actions of people, when honorable and respectful, tend to lean toward what is right and steer away from what is wrong.

In Luke 6:31, the scripture reads, "And just as you want men to do to you, you also do to them likewise."

In Matthew 7:12, the scripture reads, "Therefore, whatever you want men to do to you, do also to them, for this is the Law and the Prophets."

<u>Learning</u>

The process of learning never ends and we can all receive edification from others. By being mindful and respectful to the understanding that learning never ends we can achieve greater wisdom beyond the knowledge of which it is founded. Education not only comes from schools, but also from experiences, conversation, suffering through consequences, achieving successes, and sharing with others. There are so many avenues of learning and edification that an open mind can receive and continue to grow beyond expectations and to greater awareness.

In Proverbs 1:5 the scripture reads, "A wise man will hear and increase learning. And a man of understanding will attain wise counsel,"

In Luke 6:40, the scripture reads, "A disciple is not above his teacher, but everyone who is perfectly trained will be like his teacher."

<u>Strength</u>

Strength represents not giving up. It is the endurance to continue even when difficult times are ahead. With strength, the adversities in life will not be a hindrance to reaching goals and becoming successful. Being void of strength allows any obstacle to prevent moving forward to any success resulting in total absolute failure. To avoid failure, strength is necessary to endure and overcome obstacles put in our path. Strength is also represented by self-control to persevere and continue forth through storms in life. When considering strength needed in life consider the words endurance and self-control.

In Colossians 1:11, the scripture reads, "strengthened with all might, according to His glorious power, for all patience and longsuffering with joy;"

In Philippians 4:13, the scripture reads, "I can do all things through Christ who strengthens me."

Combination

The seventh and final pillar representing models of Excellence is a combination of the previous six. For example, to be organized, you must be disciplined. To have ethics, you must learn what is right and wrong. To be motivated, you must have strength.

One of the reasons there are seven pillars representing the models of Excellence is that the number **7** has significance. In the Book of Genesis, God created the heavens and the Earth and rested on the 7th Day. The number 7 represent something being finished or complete.

Thereafter, in the Bible, the number **7** represents a defined perfection or completion.

In no way does the Seven Pillars representing the Models of Excellence replace or make less of the nine fruits of the spirit as noted in the book of Galatians. In Galatians 5:22-23, the scripture reads, "But the fruit of the Spirit is love, joy, peace, longsuffering, kindness, goodness, faithfulness, gentleness, self-control. Against such there is no law."

Discerning Evil

wisdom and understanding

Discerning Evil

To maintain models of excellence in our lives there must be a minimal level of distraction. The ability to discern evil ensures that our wrongness found in the world we live in does not deter us from the direction necessary for us to succeed. The evil to be discerned are in the categories of deception, manipulation, and selfishness by others who may make effort to influence us. The recognition of this evil in advance will easily stomp out a possible deception, manipulation, and selfishness that others try to impose upon us.

In 1st John 4:1-3, the scripture reads, "Beloved, do not believe every spirit, but test the spirits to see whether they are from God, for many false prophets have gone out into the world. By this you know the Spirit of God: every spirit that confesses that Jesus Christ has come in the flesh is from God, and every spirit that does not confess Jesus is not from God. This is the spirit of the antichrist, which you heard was coming and now is in the world already."

<u>Deception</u>

In the Bible from the book of Proverbs chapter 6 verses 16 to 19 says "There are six things that the Lord hates, seven that are an abomination to him: haughty eyes, a lying tongue, and hands that shed innocent blood, a heart that devises wicked plans, feet that make haste to run to evil, a false witness who breathes out lies, and one who sows discord among brothers. "

In the Bible from the book of Revelations chapter 12 verse 9 says "And the great dragon was thrown down, that ancient serpent, who is called the devil and Satan, the deceiver of the whole world—he was thrown down to the earth, and his angels were thrown down with him."

In the Bible from the book of first of Timothy chapter 4 verse 1, the scripture reads: "Now the Spirit expressly says that in later times some will depart from the faith by devoting themselves to deceitful spirits and teachings of demons,"

Different evil behavior is defined as one or more of the characteristics of deception, manipulation, or operating under self-serving behavior. Self-serving behavior is selfishness.

Let us talk about deception and define what it is. Deception is the action of deceiving someone. It is action that results in deceit. Deception is fraudulent behavior involving trickery, chicanery, slyness. A bluff to give pretense of something else is a form of treachery. This deception has many purposes including manipulation and to satisfy selfishness. Manipulation and selfishness encompass two of the tree axis of evil. Deception is the third. manipulation and selfishness can result from deception. This example shows how deception, manipulation, and selfishness operate together.

The act of deception has the intent of not telling the truth. The truth is hidden. God says that the truth will set you free. With deception, there is no freedom. The difficulty from continual deception has to do with keeping the story straight for long term believability. If the story resulting from deception has no truth, the difficulty of maintaining consistency has difficulties. Fabricating a story with the intent of swaying a person's belief's or actions require continual fabrication to ensure successful deception. The person of deceit does not know how far they must act on deceiving. This behavior fails in the long term, because the discernment of fake behavior cannot last forever.

<u>Manipulation</u>

In the Bible from the book of Matthew chapter 7 verse 15, the scripture reads: "Beware of false prophets, who come to you in sheep's clothing but inwardly are ravenous wolves.

In the Bible in the book of Matthew chapter 24 verse 4, the scripture reads: And Jesus answered them, "See that no one leads you astray.

In the Bible in the book of Hebrews chapter 13 verse 8 to 9, the scripture reads: Jesus Christ is the same yesterday and today and forever. Do not be led away by diverse and strange teachings, for it is good for the heart to be strengthened by grace, not by foods, which have not benefited those devoted to them.

Manipulation involves the skillful handling or controlling something or someone. The purpose of that skillful handling may include selfishness and involves treachery, deception, and a bluff. Once again, we see how deception relates to manipulation and selfishness. The process of manipulation convinces someone to do something or think in a particular way. The method of manipulation involves pressure, force, and an act of urgency. manipulation in no way relates to a polite request unless deception is involved. Deception changes the way others think. Manipulation pushes people to do something that they would not consider themselves.

This shows that manipulation has a selfish purpose, as it does not satisfy the needs of the manipulated person or victim of manipulation.

People can be manipulated to do many things. They can be forced by threat or treachery to do something at their own expense. The manipulator saves money by pushing the expense to the one being manipulated. Other forms of manipulation involve creating a benefit to those creating the deceit for selfish reasons. Victims of manipulation receive no reward or benefit. The victims incur a cost either in money, time, property, convenience, or emotion. Manipulation creates value or convenience to a selfish deceptive person. The victim loses in the form of some value and level of convenience.

<u>Selfishness</u>

In the Bible from the book of Romans 2:8, the scripture reads: But for those who are self-seeking and do not obey the truth, but obey unrighteousness, there will be wrath and fury.

In the Bible from the book of first Corinthians chapter 10 verse 24, the scripture reads: Let no one seek his own good, but the good of his neighbor.

In the Bible from the book of Romans chapter 12 verse 3, the scripture reads: For by the grace given to me I say to everyone among you not to think of himself more highly than he ought to think, but to think with sober judgment, each according to the measure of faith that God has assigned.

Selfishness is the quality or condition of lacking consideration for others. People who are selfish concern themselves with their own profit or pleasure. Selfish people receive profit or pleasure at the expense of others. Deception and manipulation do this. Again, we see how deception, manipulation, and selfishness relate to each other.

The best ways to discern selfish behavior is to identify people who carry a high ego. People who are egocentric and egotistical show self-centered behavior identified as selfish. The resulting behavior of selfishness includes being inconsiderate, thoughtless, uncaring, uncharitable, mean, greedy, and opportunistic. This behavior satisfies selfish people with ignorance to victims of selfish behavior.

<u>Deception, Manipulation, and Selfishness</u>

In the Bible from the book of Mark chapter 7 verse 21 to 23, the scripture reads: For from within, out of the heart of man, come evil thoughts, sexual immorality, theft, murder, adultery, coveting, wickedness, deceit, sensuality, envy, slander, pride, foolishness. All these evil things come from within, and they defile a person."

In the Bible from the book of 1st of John chapter 3 verse 9 says No one born of God makes a practice of sinning, for God's seed abides in him, and he cannot keep on sinning because he has been born of God.

The word evil shares a combination of attributes of deception, manipulation, and Selfishness. Deception requires manipulation and selfishness. Manipulation requires selfishness and deception. Selfishness includes deception and manipulation. All three behaviors related to each other. With the combination of all three behaviors in motion, identifying evil behavior challenges even the more astute and intuitive person.

A way to identify evil tendencies involves breaking up the behaviors of deception, manipulation, and selfishness and identifying each one. When one is identified, then the other two can be identified by relating it to the first identified behavior. For example, an act of deception identified as a behavioral flaw. This flaw in turn relates to manipulation and selfishness. Once all three behaviors show clearly that shows evil. Identifying evil involves first identifying either deception, manipulation, or selfishness. Second, the other two behaviors show relevance to the first behavior identified.

Selfish behavior requires manipulation to deceive someone. The tendency of being selfish results in deceptive manipulation. To deceive through manipulation, require selfish behavior. Just know that evil behavior shares behaviors between deception, manipulation, and selfishness.

Integrity

A person's character is a measurement of their integrity. That character comes from a measurement of evil behavior such as deception, manipulation, and selfishness. As the Bible reminds us, we are all born into sin. We have the ability to deceive, manipulate, or have selfish tendencies. We all can improve our character by keeping a watchful eye on our levels of deception, manipulation, and selfishness. By reducing all three behaviors, our integrity greatly improves and shown in our character. Your language and behavior speak of your character.

The ways you carry yourself and speak to others speak of your character. The more positive the character, the greater a person's integrity is. Keep check on yourself. Take a close look to see, if even to a small innocent degree, if you carry traits of deception, manipulating, or selfishness.

Behavior

Poor behaviors include hypocrisy and condemnation. Hypocrisy is the practice of claiming to have moral standards or beliefs to which one's own behavior does not conform. In other words, hypocrisy is the behavior of a person condemning others for the same behavior that they possess. It is a form of deceptive behavior previously talked about. This behavior can also be used for manipulation. Hypocrisy is for selfish purposes. This means that hypocrisy or being hypocritical falls into evil behavior. People to condemn others when they themselves should share in the condemnation use hypocrisy.

<u>Love</u>

In conclusion, just know that your language and behavior speak to your character which is a measurement of your integrity. Do you want to do better? Look at the scriptures identified in this book and attend a Bible-based Christian church. Check within yourself for characteristics of deception, manipulation, and selfishness. If you can capture those three characteristics and hold them harnessed, then you will see improved behavior. Instead, look toward LOVE, as the right behavior.

LOVE = Let Our Voice Encourage

In the Bible from first Corinthians chapter 13 verses 4 to 8, it reads: Love is patient and kind; love does not envy or boast; it is not arrogant or rude. It does not insist on its own way; it is not irritable or resentful; it does not rejoice at wrongdoing but rejoices with the truth. Love bears all things, believes all things, hopes all things, endures all things. Love never ends. As for prophecies, they will pass away; as for tongues, they will cease; as for knowledge, it will pass away.

In the book of John chapter 3 verse16, it says: For God so loved the world, that he gave his only Son, that whoever believes in him should not perish but have eternal life.

David K. Ewen, M.Ed.

www.ingramcontent.com/pod-product-compliance
Lightning Source LLC
Chambersburg PA
CBHW070046260726
48658CB00002B/752